A Special Thank You!

As a special thank you for your book purchase, please log onto the following link below to
download your free colouring book to print and enjoy!

Link:

www.amazinglycoolbooks.com/specialthankyou

Copyright © 2020 Natalie Murray

My Beautiful Skin
www.amazinglycoolbooks.com

The moral right of the author has been asserted.

All rights reserved. No part of this publication may be reproduced, stored in a retrieval system, or transmitted, in any form or by any means, electronic, mechanical, photocopying, recording, or otherwise, without prior written permission from the publisher.

Illustration by Sarah-Leigh Wills.
www.happydesigner.co.uk

DMJ Publising
www.dmjpublishing.co.uk

My Beautiful Skin

Written by
Natalie Murray

Illustrations by
Happydesigner

I love my skin
I take special care of my skin.
I use special cream to moisturise my skin

I have beautiful skin that looks
very smooth
Isn't it fantastic?
Lotion is what I use!

I have great skin.
Sometimes in the winter
It goes a bit lighter.

Sometimes in the summer it goes a bit darker.
I think that's very clever.
Skin that changes with the weather.

I have very dry skin.
So, I have special cream that I use a lot.
It makes me feel better no matter what.

My skin gets itchy with little spots.
But I get a special cream when I visit
the doc's; lots of people have eczema
can you believe it?
But there are lots and lots of creams
and lotions to treat it.

We all have different shades of skin.
We will treat our skin well and not be mean.

We will wash our skin and keep it clean and moisturise it every day
Because God made us this very unique and special way

Other books in the series:

Have you got all 4?

www. amazinglycoolbooks.com

www.ingramcontent.com/pod-product-compliance
Lightning Source LLC
Chambersburg PA
CBHW081400080526
44588CB00016B/2558